To bad jokes and good food.

Welcome to "The Dad-Joke Cook Book" – a recipe for culinary pun-demonium!

Are you hungry for laughter and ready to serve up some chuckle-worthy dishes? Look no further, because this book is the perfect ingredient for your sense of humor. Get ready to cook up a storm of laughter with a side of eye-rolling. The Dad-Joke Cook Book is stuffed with groan-inducing puns, wordplay, and classic dad humor. This hilarious collection of recipes isn't just about cooking – it's a buffet of comical delights that will have you laughing all the way to the kitchen and back.

Whether you're an expert chef or a microwave maestro, this book will leave you in stitches with its witty one-liners and hilarious puns. You'll find recipes like "The Laffa-lafel," "Bun-derful Burgers," and "Omelettin' You Go." The Dad-Joke Cook Book is the perfect gift for dads, granddads, and anyone who appreciates a good laugh with their meal.

So, if you're in the mood to "taco" 'bout funny food, it's time to whisk away your woes, turn-ip the heat, and let this book guide you on a comical culinary journey that will have everyone asking for seconds – or at least a second round of jokes.

BREAKFAST

EGG-CEPTIONAL SCRAMBLE

A Fluffy and Flavorful Morning Delight

INGREDIENTS:

- 8 large eggs
- Salt and pepper, to taste
- 2 tablespoons butter
- Optional: milk, cream, or cheese

INSTRUCTIONS:

1. Crack the eggs into a bowl and beat with a fork or whisk until the yolks and whites are fully combined. For creamier eggs add a splash of milk or cream. Season with salt and pepper.

2. Heat a non-stick skillet over medium heat and add the butter. Once the butter is melted and slightly bubbly, pour in the beaten eggs.

3. Cook the eggs, gently stirring with a spatula, until they are soft and slightly set, but still a little runny. Remove from heat as the eggs will continue to cook from the residual heat.

4. Serve immediately with toast or any preferred side dish.

How do monsters like their eggs?
Terri-fried!

Why don't eggs tell jokes?
They might crack up!

What do you call an egg that goes on safari?
An eggs-plorer!

OMELETTIN' YOU GO
Fill Your Morning with Delicious Possibilities

INGREDIENTS:

- 8 large eggs

- Salt and pepper, to taste

- 2 tablespoons butter

- Your choice of fillings (e.g., cheese, diced ham, sautéed mushrooms, onions, bell peppers, tomatoes, spinach)

INSTRUCTIONS:

1. Crack 2 eggs into a bowl and beat with a fork or whisk until the yolks and whites are fully combined. Season with salt and pepper. Repeat for each omelette.

2. Heat a non-stick skillet over medium heat and add 1/2 tablespoon of butter. Once the butter is melted, pour in the beaten eggs for one omelette.

3. Cook the eggs for 2-3 minutes until they are mostly set but still slightly runny on top. Add your chosen fillings to one half of the omelette.

4. Carefully fold the omelette in half, covering the fillings, and cook for another 1-2 minutes, until fully set.

5. Gently slide the omelette onto a plate and serve. Repeat for the remaining omelettes.

How do you make an egg-roll?

You push it!

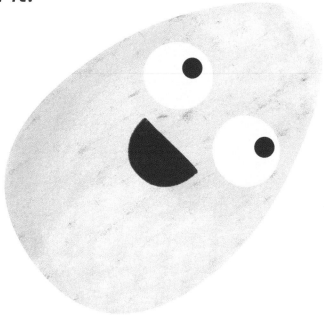

Why did the omelette join a gym?

It wanted to get egg-stra fit!

Why did the omelette go to the doctor?

It was feeling a little scrambled!

CREPE EXPECTATIONS

Sweet or Savory, Wrapped in Elegance

INGREDIENTS:

- 1 cup all-purpose flour
- 2 eggs
- 1/2 cup milk
- 1/2 cup water
- 1/4 teaspoon salt
- 2 tablespoons melted butter
- Desired fillings (e.g., Nutella, strawberries, bananas, whipped cream, ham, cheese, sautéed vegetables)

INSTRUCTIONS:

1. In a large mixing bowl, whisk together the flour and eggs. Gradually add the milk and water, stirring to combine. Add the salt and melted butter, and whisk until smooth.

2. Heat a lightly greased, non-stick skillet over medium heat. Pour about 1/4 cup of the batter into the skillet, tilting the pan to spread the batter evenly.

3. Cook the crepe for 2-3 minutes until the bottom is light golden brown. Flip and cook the other side for another 1-2 minutes.

4. Transfer the crepe to a plate and add your desired fillings. Fold the crepe in half or roll it up, and serve immediately. Repeat the process for the remaining batter to make 8 crepes, serving 2 crepes per person.

What's a crepe's favorite type of vacation?

A whisk-away weekend!

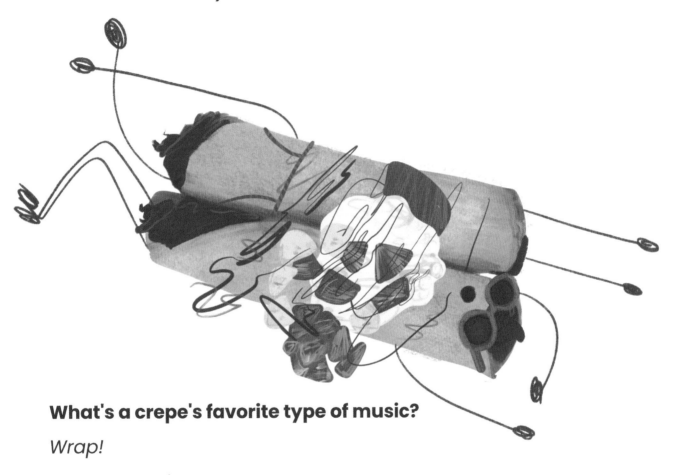

What's a crepe's favorite type of music?

Wrap!

Why did the crepe join the basketball team?

It had a great turnover rate!

SNACKS & SANDWICHES

TOMATO TANGO

Bruschetta Bites to Savor

INGREDIENTS:

- 1 baguette
- 2 cups cherry tomatoes, halved
- 1/4 cup fresh basil leaves, chopped
- 1-2 cloves garlic, minced
- 1/4 cup olive oil
- Salt and pepper, to taste
- Balsamic glaze, for drizzling (optional)

INSTRUCTIONS:

1. Preheat the oven to 400°F (200°C).
2. Slice the baguette into 1/2-inch thick slices and place them on a baking sheet. Bake for 5-6 minutes, or until lightly toasted.
3. In a medium bowl, mix together the cherry tomatoes, basil, garlic, olive oil, salt, and pepper.
4. Top each toasted baguette slice with a spoonful of the tomato mixture.
5. Drizzle with balsamic glaze, if desired, and serve immediately.

Why did the tomato turn red?

It saw the salad dressing!

Why did the bruschetta go to the party?

It wanted to be the toast of the town!

What did the tomato say to the bread?

"Stop loafing around and join me on the bruschetta!"

GRILLED CHEESE AND THANK YOU

Melty, Cheesy Comfort Food Classic

INGREDIENTS:

- 8 slices of bread
- 8 slices of cheese (e.g., cheddar, mozzarella, Monterey Jack)
- 4 tablespoons softened butter

INSTRUCTIONS:

1. Lay out 4 slices of bread and top each with 2 slices of cheese. Place another slice of bread on top to create 4 sandwiches.
2. Spread 1/2 tablespoon of softened butter on one side of each sandwich.
3. Preheat a non-stick skillet or griddle over medium heat. Place the sandwiches, butter-side down, in the skillet or griddle.
4. Cook for 3-4 minutes, until the bread is golden brown and the cheese starts to melt. Spread 1/2 tablespoon of softened butter on the uncooked side, then carefully flip the sandwiches.
5. Cook for another 3-4 minutes, until the other side is golden brown and the cheese is fully melted. Remove from heat, cut each sandwich in half, and serve immediately.

Why did the bread go to the doctor?

It was feeling a bit crumby!

What do you call a grilled cheese sandwich that's all up in your face?

Too close for comfort food!

What do you call a grilled cheese that's always late?

A procrastin-eater!

QUESA-DILLIGHTFUL
Cheesy, Customizable Mexican Snack

INGREDIENTS:

- 4 large flour tortillas
- 2 cups shredded cheese (e.g., cheddar, Monterey Jack, or Mexican blend)
- Optional fillings: cooked chicken, black beans, diced bell peppers, onions, corn, jalapeños, cooked ground beef
- 2 tablespoons vegetable oil
- Sour cream and salsa, for serving

INSTRUCTIONS:

1. Lay out the flour tortillas and sprinkle 1/2 cup of shredded cheese on one half of each tortilla. Add any optional fillings on top of the cheese.
2. Fold the tortillas in half, pressing gently to close.
3. Heat 1/2 tablespoon of vegetable oil in a non-stick skillet over medium heat. Place one folded tortilla in the skillet and cook for 2-3 minutes, until the bottom is golden brown.
4. Carefully flip the quesadilla and cook for another 2-3 minutes, until the other side is golden brown and the cheese is fully melted. Remove from heat and place on a cutting board. Repeat with the remaining tortillas.
5. Allow the quesadillas to cool for 1-2 minutes, then cut each into 3 or 4 wedges. Serve with sour cream and salsa.

What's a quesadilla's favorite day of the week?

Fry-day!

Why did the scarecrow love quesadillas?

He was always stuffed!

Why did the quesadilla become a DJ?

It knew how to spice up the party!

EMPIRE OF GREENS

The Ultimate Caesar Salad Experience

INGREDIENTS:

- 2 heads Romaine lettuce, chopped
- 2 cups cooked chicken breast, diced or shredded
- 1 cup croutons
- 1/2 cup grated Parmesan cheese
- Caesar salad dressing, to taste

INSTRUCTIONS:

1. In a large salad bowl, combine the chopped Romaine lettuce, cooked chicken breast, croutons, and grated Parmesan cheese.
2. Drizzle Caesar salad dressing over the salad, using as much or as little as desired. Toss the salad to combine and coat evenly with the dressing.
3. Serve immediately, dividing the salad among 4 plates or bowls.

What did the Caesar salad say to the crouton?

"You're my bread and butter!"

What did the lettuce say to the chicken?

Stop running, we're in this salad together!

What do you call a chicken staring at lettuce?

Chicken sees-a-salad!

FISH-TASTIC FLAVORS

The Ultimate Tuna Salad Experience

INGREDIENTS:

- 2 cans (5 oz each) tuna, drained
- 1/3 cup mayonnaise
- 1/4 cup chopped celery
- 1/4 cup chopped red onion
- 1 tablespoon Dijon mustard
- Salt and pepper, to taste
- 8 slices of bread (e.g., whole wheat, rye, or white)
- Optional: lettuce and tomato slices

INSTRUCTIONS:

1. In a medium bowl, mix together the drained tuna, mayonnaise, chopped celery, chopped red onion, Dijon mustard, salt, and pepper.
2. Lay out 4 slices of bread and evenly distribute the tuna salad mixture onto each slice. Add lettuce and tomato slices, if desired.
3. Top with the remaining bread slices to create 4 sandwiches. Cut each sandwich in half and serve immediately.

Why did the tuna blush?

Because it saw the ocean's bottom!

What's a fish's favorite musical instrument?

The bass guitar!

What's a tuna salad's favorite type of music?
Something with a catchy tuna!

MEATBALL SUB-LIME

Hearty, Saucy Italian-American Sandwich

INGREDIENTS:

- 12 pre-cooked meatballs (homemade or store-bought)
- 2 cups marinara sauce
- 4 sub rolls
- 1 cup shredded mozzarella cheese
- Optional: grated Parmesan cheese and chopped parsley for garnish

INSTRUCTIONS:

1. In a saucepan over medium heat, combine the pre-cooked meatballs and marinara sauce. Cook until the meatballs are heated through and the sauce is bubbling, about 10-15 minutes.
2. While the meatballs are heating, preheat the oven to 350°F (175°C). Slice the sub rolls lengthwise without cutting all the way through, creating a pocket for the meatballs.
3. Place 3 meatballs and some sauce into each sub roll. Top with a generous amount of shredded mozzarella cheese.
4. Place the meatball subs on a baking sheet and bake for 5-7 minutes, or until the cheese is melted and bubbly.
5. Remove from the oven, garnish with grated Parmesan cheese and chopped parsley if desired, and serve immediately.

Why did the meatball keep telling jokes?

It wanted to be on a roll!

Why did the meatball go to the gym?

To beef up!

Why did the meatball go to the doctor?
It was feeling a little saucy!

SLOPPY JOMENTUM

Tasty, Nostalgic Homemade Favorite

INGREDIENTS:

- 1 lb ground beef
- 1 small onion, chopped
- 1 small green bell pepper, chopped
- 1 cup ketchup
- 2 tablespoons brown sugar
- 2 tablespoons Worcestershire sauce
- 1 tablespoon yellow mustard
- Salt and pepper, to taste
- 4 hamburger buns

INSTRUCTIONS:

1. In a large skillet over medium heat, cook the ground beef, onion, and green bell pepper until the beef is browned and the vegetables are tender. Drain any excess grease.
2. Stir in the ketchup, brown sugar, Worcestershire sauce, mustard, salt, and pepper. Simmer the mixture for 10-15 minutes, stirring occasionally.
3. While the mixture simmers, toast the hamburger buns if desired.
4. Divide the Sloppy Joe mixture evenly among the bottom halves of the hamburger buns. Top with the other halves and serve immediately.

Why did the Sloppy Joe go to school?

To get a little breader at math!

Why did the Sloppy Joe get in trouble?

It couldn't keep itself together!

What do you call a sloppy joe that's a great golfer?

A hole-in-bun!

DINNER

SPAGHETTI A-GLEE-O E OLIO
Simple, Garlic-Infused Pasta Perfection

INGREDIENTS:

- 1 lb spaghetti
- 6-7 garlic cloves, thinly sliced
- 2/3 cup olive oil
- 1/2 teaspoon red pepper flakes
- 1/2 teaspoon of thyme
- Salt and pepper, to taste
- Chopped parsley and grated Parmesan cheese, for garnish

INSTRUCTIONS:

1. Cook the spaghetti in a pot of boiling salted water according to package directions until al dente. Reserve 1 cup of pasta water before draining.
2. In a large skillet, heat the olive oil over medium heat. Add the garlic and cook until golden, about 2 minutes.
3. Add the red pepper flakes and thyme and cook for another 30 seconds. Turn off the heat.
4. Add the cooked spaghetti to the skillet, along with a splash of the reserved pasta water. Toss well to combine, adding more pasta water if necessary to create a silky sauce. Season with salt and pepper.
5. Serve immediately, garnished with chopped parsley and grated Parmesan cheese.m halves of the hamburger buns. Top with the other halves and serve immediately.

What do you call a fake noodle?

An impasta!

What did the pasta say to the tomato?

Don't get saucy with me!

Why was the pasta always late?
It lost track of thyme.

ZITI-LICIOUS BAKE
A Cheesy, Comforting Crowd-Pleaser

INGREDIENTS:

- 1 lb ziti pasta
- 2 cups marinara sauce
- 1 1/2 cups ricotta cheese
- 2 cups shredded mozzarella cheese
- 1 cup grated Parmesan cheese
- Salt and pepper, to taste

INSTRUCTIONS:

1. Preheat the oven to 350ºF (175ºC). Cook the ziti pasta in a pot of boiling salted water according to package directions until al dente. Drain and set aside.
2. In a large bowl, mix the cooked ziti with the marinara sauce, ricotta cheese, half of the mozzarella cheese, and half of the Parmesan cheese. Season with salt and pepper.
3. Pour the pasta mixture into a 9x13-inch baking dish. Top with the remaining mozzarella and Parmesan cheeses.
4. Bake for 25-30 minutes, or until the cheese is melted and bubbly. Remove from the oven and let stand for a few minutes before serving.

Why did the tomato sauce go to the spa?

To get rid of its ziti.

What did the baked ziti ask the pasta when it wanted a second opinion?

"Penne for your thoughts?"

What do you call a ziti that speaks multiple languages?

A linguine-ist!

PASTABLY PRIMAVERA
Colorful, Fresh, and Veggie-Packed Pasta

INGREDIENTS:

- 1 lb pasta (e.g., penne, farfalle, or fettuccine)
- 2 cups chopped fresh vegetables (e.g., bell peppers, zucchini, cherry tomatoes, asparagus, or broccoli)
- 3 tablespoons olive oil
- 3 cloves garlic, minced
- 1/2 cup vegetable broth
- 1/2 cup grated Parmesan cheese
- Salt and pepper, to taste

INSTRUCTIONS:

1. Cook the pasta in a pot of boiling salted water according to package directions until al dente. Drain and set aside.
2. In a large skillet, heat the olive oil over medium heat. Add the garlic and cook for 1-2 minutes, until fragrant.
3. Add the chopped vegetables and cook for 5-7 minutes, until tender but still crisp. Stir in the vegetable broth and cook for another 2-3 minutes.
4. Add the cooked pasta to the skillet and toss to combine. Stir in the Parmesan cheese and season with salt and pepper.
5. Serve immediately, with additional Parmesan cheese if desired.

Why did the pasta need a break?

It was feeling a little drained.

What's the best way to repress a bad memory?

Spaghet-about-it.

How do you fix a broken pasta?
With tomato paste.

CHICK-A-LFREDO FETTUCCINE

Creamy, Decadent Pasta Dinner

INGREDIENTS:

- 1 lb fettuccine pasta
- 2 cups cooked chicken breast, diced or shredded
- 1 cup heavy cream
- 1/2 cup unsalted butter
- 1 cup grated Parmesan cheese
- Salt and pepper, to taste
- Chopped parsley, for garnish

INSTRUCTIONS:

1. Cook the fettuccine pasta in a pot of boiling salted water according to package directions until al dente. Drain and set aside.
2. In a large skillet or saucepan, heat the heavy cream and butter over medium-low heat until the butter has melted and the mixture is warm. Stir in the grated Parmesan cheese until smooth and creamy.
3. Add the cooked fettuccine and chicken to the skillet and toss to combine, making sure the pasta and chicken are evenly coated with the sauce. Season with salt and pepper.
4. Serve immediately, garnished with chopped parsley.

What do you call a pasta that's always scared?

Fettuccini Afraid-o.

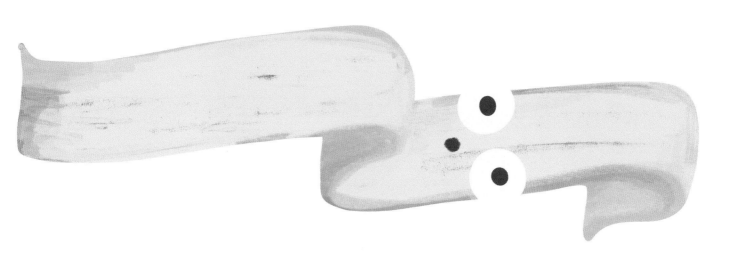

Why do chickens love Italian food?

Because of their peckish appetite!

What's a chicken's favorite type of pasta?
Fowl-fredo!

BBQ CHICKEN PIZZ-AZZ

Sweet, Tangy, and Smoky Pizza Night

INGREDIENTS:

- 1 lb pizza dough (store-bought or homemade)
- 1/2 cup BBQ sauce
- 1 1/2 cups cooked chicken breast, diced or shredded
- 1/2 small red onion, thinly sliced
- 1 1/2 cups shredded mozzarella cheese
- 1/4 cup chopped fresh cilantro

INSTRUCTIONS:

1. Preheat the oven to 475°F (245°C). Roll out the pizza dough on a lightly floured surface into a 12-inch circle or desired shape.
2. Transfer the rolled-out dough to a pizza stone or baking sheet. Spread the BBQ sauce evenly over the dough, leaving a small border around the edges.
3. Top the sauce with the cooked chicken, red onion slices, and shredded mozzarella cheese.
4. Bake the pizza for 12-15 minutes, or until the crust is golden brown and the cheese is melted and bubbly.
5. Remove the pizza from the oven and let it cool for a few minutes. Sprinkle with chopped fresh cilantro, slice, and serve.

Why did the pizza chef quit his job?

He kneaded a change.

What's a pizza's favorite type of music?

Hip-pop-eroni!

What's a pizza maker's favorite dance move?

The saucy spin!

TACO 'BOUT BEEF

Spiced, Satisfying, and Family-Friendly Mexican Classic

INGREDIENTS:

- 1 lb ground beef
- 1 small onion, chopped
- 1 packet taco seasoning
- 1/2 cup water
- 8 taco shells (hard or soft)
- Toppings: shredded lettuce, diced tomatoes, shredded cheese, sour cream, and salsa

INSTRUCTIONS:

1. In a large skillet over medium heat, cook the ground beef and onion until the beef is browned and the onion is tender. Drain any excess grease.
2. Stir in the taco seasoning and water. Bring the mixture to a boil, then reduce the heat and simmer for 5-10 minutes, or until the sauce has thickened.
3. While the beef mixture is simmering, prepare the taco shells according to package directions.
4. To assemble the tacos, fill each shell with the beef mixture and desired toppings. Serve immediately.

What do you call a group of beef tacos that ring?

The Taco Bells!

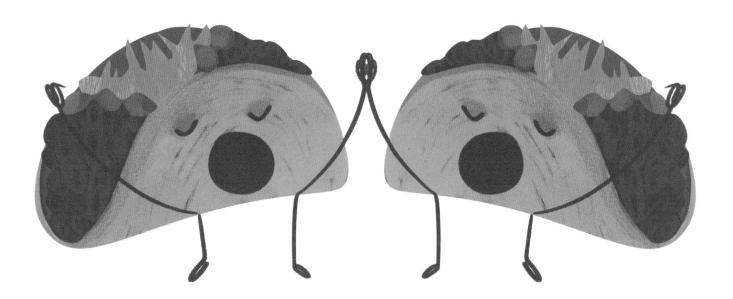

What do you call a spooky beef taco?

A Tac-o-lantern.

How do you know if a beef taco is a great writer?
It uses lots of meat-aphors.

FISH TACO-FINITY

Crispy, Flavorful, and Seafood-Sensation Tacos

INGREDIENTS:

- 1 lb white fish fillets (e.g., cod, tilapia, or halibut)
- 1/2 cup flour
- Salt and pepper, to taste
- 1/2 cup vegetable oil
- 8 small flour or corn tortillas
- Toppings: shredded cabbage, diced avocado, sliced radishes, and lime wedges
- Optional: tartar sauce or salsa

INSTRUCTIONS:

1. Pat the fish fillets dry with paper towels and cut them into 1-2 inch wide strips. Season the flour with salt and pepper, and then dredge the fish strips in the flour, shaking off any excess.
2. In a large skillet, heat the vegetable oil over medium-high heat. Fry the fish strips in batches for 2-3 minutes per side, or until golden brown and cooked through. Transfer the cooked fish to a paper towel-lined plate to drain any excess oil.
3. Warm the tortillas in the microwave or on a hot skillet for about 30 seconds, until they are soft and pliable.
4. To assemble the tacos, place a piece of fried fish on each tortilla and add desired toppings. Serve with lime wedges and optional tartar sauce or salsa.

Why did the fish go to Hollywood?

It wanted to be a starfish!

Why are fish so smart?

Because they live in schools!

How do you know if a fish taco will change the world?

It has a lot of fish-ionary ideas.

FAJITA FIESTA

Sizzling, Colorful, and Fun Mexican Dinner

INGREDIENTS:

- 1 lb chicken or beef, thinly sliced
- 1 large bell pepper, sliced
- 1 large onion, sliced
- 2 tablespoons vegetable oil
- 1 packet fajita seasoning
- 8 small flour or corn tortillas
- Toppings: sour cream, guacamole, shredded cheese, and salsa

INSTRUCTIONS:

1. In a large skillet, heat 1 tablespoon of vegetable oil over medium-high heat. Add the sliced chicken or beef and cook until browned and cooked through. Remove from the skillet and set aside.
2. Add the remaining tablespoon of vegetable oil to the skillet, and cook the bell pepper and onion slices until tender and slightly charred.
3. Return the cooked meat to the skillet, and add the fajita seasoning. Stir well to combine and cook for another 2-3 minutes.
4. Warm the tortillas in the microwave or on a hot skillet for about 30 seconds, until they are soft and pliable.
5. To serve, place the meat and vegetable mixture on a serving platter alongside the warmed tortillas and desired toppings. Let everyone assemble their own fajitas.

How do you make a fajita smile?

You taco 'bout a good time.

Why do fajitas make great detectives?

They always get to the meat of the matter!

What do tortillas sing at birthday parties
Fajita jolly good fellow.

VEGGIE FRIED RICE OF PASSAGE

Flavorful, Easy, and Veggie-Filled Fried Rice

INGREDIENTS:

- 3 cups cooked white or brown rice (preferably a day old)
- 1 cup frozen mixed vegetables (e.g., peas, carrots, corn, and green beans)
- 2 large eggs, beaten
- 2 tablespoons vegetable oil
- 2 green onions, thinly sliced
- 2 tablespoons soy sauce
- Salt and pepper, to taste

INSTRUCTIONS:

1. In a large skillet or wok, heat 1 tablespoon of vegetable oil over medium-high heat. Add the beaten eggs and scramble until fully cooked. Transfer the eggs to a plate and set aside.
2. In the same skillet, heat the remaining tablespoon of vegetable oil. Add the frozen mixed vegetables and cook for 3-4 minutes, or until heated through.
3. Stir in the cooked rice and soy sauce, mixing well to combine. Cook for another 2-3 minutes, allowing the rice to get slightly crispy.
4. Add the scrambled eggs back to the skillet and stir to combine. Season with salt and pepper, and garnish with sliced green onions before serving.

What did the rice say to the veggies?

"Lettuce be friends!"

Why do vegetables love fried rice?

It's a rice way to meet new friends!

What do you call a vegetable that plays the drums?

A beet master!

CHICKEN STIR-FRIDAY
Quick, Flavorful, and Wok-Tossed Dinner

INGREDIENTS:

- 1 lb boneless, skinless chicken breasts, cut into thin strips
- 2 cups mixed vegetables (e.g., bell peppers, broccoli, carrots, and snap peas)
- 3 tablespoons vegetable oil
- 1/4 cup soy sauce
- 1 tablespoon cornstarch
- 1/2 cup chicken broth
- 2 cloves garlic, minced
- Salt and pepper, to taste
- Cooked white or brown rice, for serving

INSTRUCTIONS:

1. In a small bowl, whisk together the soy sauce, cornstarch, and chicken broth. Set aside.
2. In a large skillet or wok, heat 2 tablespoons of vegetable oil over medium-high heat. Add the chicken strips and cook until browned and cooked through. Transfer the cooked chicken to a plate and set aside.
3. Add the remaining tablespoon of vegetable oil to the skillet, along with the minced garlic. Cook for 1 minute, until fragrant.
4. Add the mixed vegetables to the skillet and cook for 4-5 minutes, or until tender-crisp.
5. Return the cooked chicken to the skillet and pour in the soy sauce mixture. Stir well to combine and cook for another 2-3 minutes, until the sauce has thickened.
6. Season with salt and pepper, and serve the chicken stir-fry over cooked rice.

What do you call a vegetable that practices martial arts?

A Brocco-lee!

Why did the chicken join the stir-fry band?

It wanted to play the wok and roll!

Why was the chicken so good at basketball?

It had a great wing span!

44

SHRIMPLY SCAMPI
Buttery, Garlicky Seafood Pasta

INGREDIENTS:

- 1 lb large shrimp, peeled and deveined
- 1/2 cup unsalted butter
- 4 cloves garlic, minced
- 1/2 cup white wine or chicken broth
- 1/4 cup fresh lemon juice
- Salt and pepper, to taste
- Chopped parsley and grated Parmesan cheese, for garnish
- Cooked linguine or angel hair pasta, for serving

INSTRUCTIONS:

1. In a large skillet, melt the butter over medium heat. Add the minced garlic and cook for 1-2 minutes, until fragrant.
2. Add the shrimp to the skillet and cook for 2-3 minutes per side, until they turn pink and are cooked through. Remove the cooked shrimp from the skillet and set aside.
3. Pour the white wine or chicken broth and lemon juice into the skillet, and bring to a simmer. Cook for 2-3 minutes, until the sauce has slightly reduced.
4. Return the cooked shrimp to the skillet and toss to coat with the sauce. Season with salt and pepper.
5. Serve the shrimp scampi over cooked pasta, garnished with chopped parsley and grated Parmesan cheese.

What's a shrimp's favorite type of party?

A shell-ebration!

Why did the shrimp not want to share it's garlic?

She was too shellfish.

What's a shrimp's favorite type of jewelry?

A coral-ful necklace!

BUN-DERFUL BURGERS

Customizable, Grill-Ready Delights

INGREDIENTS:

- 1 lb ground beef
- 1/2 cup breadcrumbs
- 1/4 cup grated onion
- 1 large egg
- 1/4 cup ketchup
- Salt and pepper, to taste
- 4 hamburger buns
- Toppings: lettuce, tomato, onion, cheese, pickles, and condiments

INSTRUCTIONS:

1. In a large mixing bowl, combine the ground beef, breadcrumbs, grated onion, egg, ketchup, salt, and pepper. Mix until well combined.
2. Divide the mixture into 4 equal portions and shape each portion into a burger patty.
3. Preheat a grill or skillet over medium heat. Cook the burger patties for 4-5 minutes per side, or until cooked to your desired level of doneness. If adding cheese, place a slice on each patty during the last minute of cooking.
4. Toast the hamburger buns on the grill or skillet for about 1 minute, or until lightly browned.
5. Assemble the burgers with the cooked patties, desired toppings, and condiments. Serve immediately.

What did the burger say to the audience?

Lettuce entertain you!

Why did the burger go to the gym?

It wanted better buns!

What do you call a burger that can play the piano?
A bereft-oven!

CHICKEN FINGERS, HONEY, MUSTARD BE LOVE

Crispy, Dippable, and Kid-Friendly Treats

INGREDIENTS:

- 1 lb boneless, skinless chicken breasts, cut into strips
- 1 cup all-purpose flour
- 1/2 teaspoon salt
- 1/4 teaspoon black pepper
- 2 large eggs, beaten
- 2 cups breadcrumbs
- Vegetable oil, for frying
- Honey Mustard Sauce: 1/4 cup honey, 1/4 cup Dijon mustard, 2 tablespoons mayonnaise

INSTRUCTIONS:

1. In a shallow dish, combine the flour, salt, and pepper. Place the beaten eggs in another shallow dish, and the breadcrumbs in a third shallow dish.
2. Dredge each chicken strip first in the flour mixture, then in the beaten eggs, and finally in the breadcrumbs, pressing to ensure even coating.
3. Heat about 1 inch of vegetable oil in a deep skillet over medium heat. Fry the breaded chicken strips in batches for 3-4 minutes per side, or until golden brown and cooked through. Use a slotted spoon to transfer the cooked chicken fingers to a paper towel-lined plate to drain any excess oil.
4. To make the honey mustard sauce, whisk together the honey, Dijon mustard, and mayonnaise in a small bowl.
5. Serve the chicken fingers with the honey mustard sauce for dipping.

Why did the chicken finger go to the party with the onion rings?

Because they're batter together.

What's a chicken finger's favorite TV show?

Breaking Bread.

Did you know can pay bills with chicken strips?

They're considered legal "tender".

CHILI CON CARNE-VAL

Spicy, Hearty, and Slow-Simmered Comfort Food

INGREDIENTS:

- 1 lb ground beef
- 1 large onion, chopped
- 2 cloves garlic, minced
- 1 can (15 oz) kidney beans, drained and rinsed
- 1 can (15 oz) diced tomatoes
- 1 can (8 oz) tomato sauce
- 2 tablespoons chili powder
- 1 teaspoon ground cumin
- 1 teaspoon salt
- 1/2 teaspoon black pepper
- Optional toppings: shredded cheese, sour cream, chopped green onions, and tortilla chips

INSTRUCTIONS:

1. In a large pot or Dutch oven, brown the ground beef over medium heat, breaking it up with a spoon as it cooks. Once browned, remove any excess fat.
2. Add the chopped onion and minced garlic to the pot, and cook for 5-7 minutes, or until the onion is softened.
3. Stir in the kidney beans, diced tomatoes, tomato sauce, chili powder, cumin, salt, and pepper. Bring the mixture to a simmer, then reduce the heat to low and cover the pot.
4. Cook the chili for at least 30 minutes, stirring occasionally. The longer it cooks, the more the flavors will meld together.
5. Serve the chili in bowls with desired toppings.

What's a chili's favorite pop band?

Spice Girls!

What do you call chili that's not yours?

Nacho chili!

Why don't chefs ever tell secrets in the kitchen?

Because the chili might spill the beans!

THE LAFFA-LAFEL

Crispy, Flavorful, and Middle Eastern Delight

INGREDIENTS:

- 2 cups canned chickpeas, drained and rinsed
- 1 small onion, chopped
- 2 cloves garlic, minced
- 1/4 cup fresh parsley, chopped
- 1 teaspoon ground cumin
- 1 teaspoon ground coriander
- 1/2 teaspoon salt
- 1/4 teaspoon black pepper
- 1/4 teaspoon baking soda
- Vegetable oil, for frying
- Pita bread, for serving
- Toppings: lettuce, tomato, cucumber, and tahini sauce

INSTRUCTIONS:

1. In a food processor, combine the chickpeas, onion, garlic, parsley, cumin, coriander, salt, pepper, and baking soda. Pulse until a coarse mixture is formed, scraping down the sides of the bowl as needed.
2. Shape the chickpea mixture into 12 equal-sized balls or patties.
3. Heat about 1 inch of vegetable oil in a deep skillet over medium heat. Fry the falafel balls in batches for 2-3 minutes per side, or until golden brown and crispy. Use a slotted spoon to transfer the cooked falafel to a paper towel-lined plate to drain any excess oil.
4. To serve, stuff the falafel into pita bread with desired toppings and drizzle with tahini sauce.

Why do chickpeas never start arguments?

They're all about that peas-ful life!

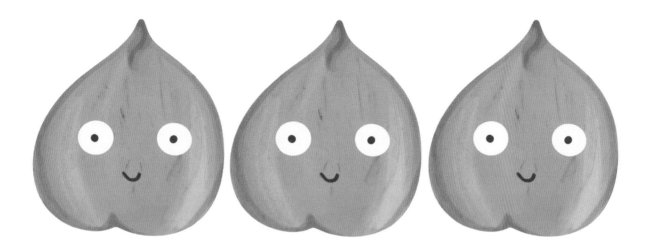

What's a falafel's favorite dance?

The chickpea-cha!

Why did the chickpea refuse to fight?
It didn't want to start a falafel!

BONUS
DAD JOKES

- **Why did the spatula become a detective?** It wanted to get to the bottom of every case!

- **What do you call a lazy whisk?** A slow stirrer!

- **Why did the colander become a therapist?** It's great at helping people strain out their problems!

- **What do you call a nervous knife?** A bit on edge!

- **Why did the spoon join the band?** It was great at stirring up some tunes!

- **What do you call a pot that's always getting into trouble?** A hot mess!

- **Why did the can opener break up with the can?** It just couldn't handle the pressure anymore!

- **What do you call a ladle that works in in middle management?** A soupervisor!

- **Why did the measuring cup go to culinary school?** It wanted to be a well-rounded utensil!

- **Why did the peeler start a career in fashion?** It was great at stripping down to the essentials!

- **What do you call a pastry brush that's always late?** A tardy baster!

Printed in Great Britain
by Amazon